The Place I Call Home

Other Books by Maria Mazziotti Gillan

The Place I Call Home

Maria Mazziotti Gillan

The New York Quarterly Foundation, Inc.
New York, New York

NYQ Books™ is an imprint of The New York Quarterly Foundation, Inc.

The New York Quarterly Foundation, Inc.
P. O. Box 2015
Old Chelsea Station
New York, NY 10113

www.nyqbooks.org

First Edition

Set in New Baskerville

Layout and Design by Raymond P. Hammond
Cover illustration by Linda Hillringhouse | www.hillringhouseart.com
Photograph of author provided by Joseph Costa | www.joecphoto.com

Library of Congress Control Number: 2012933645

ISBN: 978-1-935520-67-2

The Place I Call Home

Acknowledgments

Grateful acknowledgments to the editors of the following journals in which these poems, sometimes in early versions, first appeared or are forthcoming: "My Mother Used to Wash My Hair," *Tiferet: A Journal of Spiritual Literature*, 2011; "My Mother's 1950s Refrigerator," "My Brother Stands in the Snow, 1947, Paterson, NJ," and "When I Was Young We Played," *Paddlefish*, 2012; "Even When We Didn't Have Money," *Paddlefish*, 2009; "My Mother Used to Iron" and "How Spring Turns," *Louisiana Literature*, 2007; "I Grew Up with Tom Mix," *Paddlefish*, 2007; "The Tin Ball and the War Effort," *Caduceus*, 2010; "In Second Grade," *CT River Review*, 2010; "My Fifth Grade Teacher Miss Spinelli" and "Festival at Northern Valley High School," Special Edition of *Solo Café*, 2012; "Graduating from PS No. 18," "All His Life My Father Worked in Factories," and "The Little General," *Connecticut Review*, 2012; "So Much That Is Not Right with the World,"*San Diego Poetry Annual*, 2011/2012; "Girls," "My Mother Only Went to Third Grade in San Mauro," and "Doing the Twist with Bobby Darin," *Lips*, 2008/2009; "The Cedar Keepsake Box," *Rattle*, 2009; "A Few Years Ago, I Moved You Out of Our Bedroom" and "The Bratz Dolls Outpace Barbie," *New York Quarterly*; "The Other Night, You Came Home," *Pennsylvania English*, 2010; "All Morning in the September Light," *Lips* 2007/2008; "April Snowstorm" and "Calling My Mother Back from the Dead," *OCHO*, 2007; "How Do I Pack Up the House of My Life?" *The Cartographer Electric*, 2008; "Jacobs Department Store" and "I Was Thinking about Distances," *Connecticut Review*, 2009; "A Poem about a Turnip," *Edison Literary Review*, 2011; "In My Dream, the Light" and "When I Speak Sometimes," *Voices in Italian Americana*, 2011; "The Boys Call My Grandson Names," *Provincetown Arts Journal*, 2008/2009; "In These Green Mountains" and "The Ducks Walk across River Street in Paterson," *Tiferet: A Journal of Spiritual Literature*, 2010.

for my mother, Angelina Schiavo Mazziotti
who taught us how to love unconditionally

and
for my daughter, Jennifer,
who is the light in every room she enters

Contents

The Place I Call Home

That Sound Carries Me toward Childhood

It is dark. I swear I hear my mother calling, though it is
fifteen years since she died and more than fifty years
since we lived in the 17th Street apartment that I think of
when I think of my childhood, that two-family house
with its back stoop where all the neighborhood kids joined us

when my mother called us home. In the back yard,
Zio Guillermo's garden flourished, with its corn stalks taller
than any of us, its vines heavy with ripe tomatoes, the air
tangy with herbs, rosemary, oregano, and mint and the tart
aroma of zucchini and eggplant. Behind the screen door,

I imagine I can still see my mother cleaning up the supper
dishes and starting to cook food for the next day so it would
be ready when she came home from the factory where she
worked. When I think of that place and time, it is lit with
fireflies we captured in glass jars. We poked holes in the jars

so the fireflies wouldn't die and the sky, deep as black
velvet, was crammed with stars. Then my mother would call
us into the lit kitchen, and the three of us, my brother, sister,
and I would have milk with Bosco in it and cookies
my mother baked. With the radio on to one of the programs

we listened to, the Lone Ranger or the Shadow, we'd play
Monopoly and dominoes and my father would open his hand
and inside would be a chocolate for each of us. Looking
back, I see how safe I was then, nothing could harm me,
my parents spinning a world for us that would always warm

us, no matter how many years went by, and though my mother
and father and sister are all dead, and my brother, the doctor,
has hair that's turned suddenly white, and I am shocked to see
how old I look, as long as I can hear my mother calling me home,
as long as we can sit in memory at the oilcloth covered table,
the dangling fixture painting our faces with light,
I am loved as I was then.

My Mother Used to Wash My Hair

When my mother used to wash my hair,
she'd scrub so hard I was sure she wanted
to scalp me. Then she'd wrap my hair in white rags
to make it curl. Me in my sausage curls, my shiny hair,
my big serious sad eyes. That was on 17th Street.

I was seven and skinny. I wanted to be beautiful,
except that all the wanting in the world couldn't make it true.
Books were the boats that carried me away from the skin
I was born in. Words sparkled like stars. The stories
Miss Ferraro read to us live in my mind, a private music.

Memories stay with me—the feel of a book in my hands,
the sunlit windows of the Riverside branch of the public library,
the sound of poems read aloud in the classrooms
of PS No. 18. Those classrooms suddenly filled with light,
like the light that glows in the huge red disk of the sun

above the hills this morning, the broken world
still filled with so much surprising grace.

My Mother's 1950s Refrigerator

My mother had this 1950s refrigerator, the kind
with the small freezer built inside where the ice
would build up like stalagmites and the motor
would whir when it signaled that the temperature
inside was going up. My mother earned her living
with a needle. Sometimes we'd play around her
when she sewed in the old brown rocker,
the basting threads piling like clouds around her.

We pretended we were jumping off cliffs when we'd climb
on the arm of the sofa and jump off, though we'd jump
quietly so she wouldn't know, because children
were supposed to be seen and not heard. The twenty-five
cents an hour that she earned provided the pennies
she'd give us to buy cones at Burke's ice cream parlor.
I think sometimes of the cartons of blueberries I buy
at $3.95 a pint and remember my mother's refrigerator
that was always full of homemade food—bread, meatballs,
braciola, spinach, broccoli rabe, but no blueberries,
this small berry I didn't taste until I was a grown woman
and married myself, and I imagine my mother's horror
at the thought of her spoiled daughter paying $3.95 a pint
for blueberries just because she wants them.

My Brother Stands in the Snow, 1947, Paterson, NJ

Fifty years later, my brother is still my baby brother.
I imagine him in his woolen winter coat, tan-colored,
that with his sallow face made him look dead,
and his woolen hat that matched the coat. It had ear
flaps that snapped under his chin. He is about four
and looks wide-eyed and sweet and even then,
self-contained. I can see him standing in the snow.

It is 1947, that huge snowstorm where the snow is piled
almost to my chest. Even fifty years later, my brother
who has now been a doctor for more than thirty years,
is still my baby brother. Though he is my doctor, though I
admire and love him, though his hair has turned gray,
I can hear my mother's voice telling me to watch out
for him, as my sister watched out for me,
so that even today, I can't help worrying about him,

can't help reaching up to smooth down his thinning gray
hair when it is rumpled and fly-away, as though he were still
that little boy whose hair I combed so carefully, wetting
the comb first and parting the hair as my mother taught me
so he'd look good when people saw him on the street
where I dragged him behind me, held his hand
and scolded him as we walked.

Even When We Didn't Have Money

At Easter, my mother bought us each an outfit. My brother a blue suit,
blue tie, white shirt and dress shoes, and my sister and I,
pastel dresses bought on sale the previous year, bought two sizes
too big to make sure they'd fit us the next Easter, those leftover
Easter dresses that would be out of style.

We wore them to Blessed Sacrament Church on Easter and we visited
after Mass to show off our dressed up selves, me, in my pastel fake
straw hat with its fake flowers and stiff pale netting, my face long
as a horse's, my skin too dark, and foreign-looking for pale pink or light blue.

In all those Easter pictures, I am skinny and awkward, my eyes
huge and sad, but that's not the way I remember it:
my sister, brother and I going to Zia Antoinetta's house where we
were given a dollar apiece and fancy cookies to eat and cream soda.
We'd stay awhile and then walk

down 18th Street to Zia Louisa's house where she'd give us
chocolate pieces broken off from a huge Hershey bar she kept
in her china closet and jelly glasses of milk, and up 4th Avenue
to Zia Rosa's where we'd get another dollar apiece
and small chocolate Easter eggs, and then finally back home

where my mother had been cooking all morning and the aroma
of roasted chicken and potatoes, gravy and meatballs, and home baked
bread filled the air and my father, who loved surprises, would give us
each a chocolate bunny which we hoarded and ate a little bit at a time.

How little it took to make us happy. Today, thinking of my sister, dead now
four years, my brother whose voice on the phone sounds forlorn,
though he is a successful doctor with a wife and children who love him,
and myself, that child in her too big dresses, her plastic patent leather
shoes, her blistered feet, turned into this woman who tells

the truth when her children ask her what she wants for Christmas,
says, "I don't want anything. I don't need anything,"
just as her mother did.

17

Now I see what my mother meant, how the huge longing
we carry when we are young disappears as we grow
older, and in its place, gratitude for the momentary grace
of sun on the brick buildings, pale autumn light in the courtyard,
the mountains in the distance that appear to touch the grayish blue
of the November sky.

My Mother Used to Iron

My mother used to iron our clothes while she listened
to the radio. We listened with her gathered around
the kitchen table in the 17th Street kitchen with its huge,
black coal stove. She'd wash our clothes
on the scrub board because she couldn't afford
a washing machine. She was paying fifty cents
a week toward a wringer washer at Quackenbush's
Department Store. She still had a lot of payments
to make, but she'd scrub our clothes, hand-me-downs
from Zia Christina's daughter, and then, dip them in a bowl
of starch. The starch was a powder that would turn blue
when it was mixed with water or am I remembering it all wrong?
It was so long ago,

my brother, sister and I sitting at the table, listening
to the radio. *Stella Dallas* and *The Lone Ranger*
and *The Shadow*, my mother with the black iron heating up
on the stove. When the iron would cool off, she'd put it back
on the stove and use another one that had been heating up there.
The clothes were so clean and crisp-looking when she finished,
one hundred percent cotton, stiff with starch and the hot press
of the iron.

Years later, when my own children were growing up
and their clothes, though permanent press, were always a little
crumpled looking, limp and loose. Sometimes, if I forgot them
in the dryer, they'd be wrinkled. I'd have to wash them
all over again. My mother would berate me for being slovenly.
"How could you send your children out like that?
When you were growing up, your clothes
were always all pressed and starched.
I bought you an iron," she'd say,
and I'd bite my lip to keep from saying,

"Yes, we were clean and our clothes were starched,
but the house was always so neat it felt untouchable.
We always had to sit with our feet on the floor, or hands

19

in our laps, not touching the arms of the chair," though that's unfair,
as I suppose my own children will be unfair to me, because
I'm leaving out how much she loved us, how every bit
of cooking and cleaning she did was for us, how she never
bought anything for herself but always found the money
for a pretty dress for me, how the things I gave

to my own children, freedom to have a house full of friends,
to jump on the furniture, to be silly with them, make
funny faces, my house full of dust balls
and toys and books, might not be
the house my children wanted,
the mother they thought I should have been.
We all try to make up for what we didn't get
or what we thought we needed. We try to give
our children what we missed, even if
that wasn't what they wanted at all.

I Grew Up with Tom Mix

I grew up with Tom Mix and Roy Rogers, Hopalong Cassidy,
the Lone Ranger and Tonto. The good guys always wore white hats
so it was easy to tell them from the bad guys. Little boys had cap
guns and six shooters with holsters. Some of the boys

even wore cowboy vests and boots. We listened to the brown
counter top radio, made of imitation mahogany, tan netting
over its speakers. We'd pull kitchen chairs up to the counter
on the built-in china closet, and in the kitchen,

heated by a huge black iron coal stove, we'd listen to the programs.
We had to imagine their horses, their white hats, miles of open
space and mountain ranges we had never seen, our imaginations
filling in the gaps left by whatever we didn't know, the places

we'd never been. The radio let us leave behind that Paterson
apartment, transported us to the great valleys of the West,
to covered wagons, the saloons, the shootouts on dirty, unpaved
streets. Our real world had boundaries built by my Italian parents

and the streets we were allowed to travel, the Riverside Oval
on one end and 4th Avenue and Mastalia's grocery store
and Burke's candy store on the other, and in between, the children
we played with each day. But huddled near the radio we could go

anywhere, be anyone, imagine lives so different from our own,
exciting and dangerous, where at the end of each program
we knew no hero we loved and admired ever died.

The Tin Ball and the War Effort

Zio Guillermo worked in a silk factory in Paterson for 40 years.
He was tall and slender and patrician, his thick gray hair
perfectly shaped, though he went to the barber on 16th Street
and 5th Avenue, and not a fancy stylist. Zio Guillermo married
Zia Louisa, my honorary aunt, when they were in their 40s.

Zio Guillermo was Zia Louisa's fourth husband.
All the others died. You'd think that would have given him pause.
They lived in a second floor apartment in the tenement
on 17th Street; we lived on the first floor. Zio Guillermo
was my Godfather, and treated me like the child he never had.

When they'd visit, he and my father would talk politics. They both
adored FDR. They drank anisette in small glasses and espresso
in tiny cups with tiny spoons to stir in the sugar. My uncle
would give me a drop of espresso and sugar in a glass of milk.

He smoked Camels, three packs a day. I always think of him
with smoke curling around him, letting me help him remove
the tin foil from his cigarette packs and together we'd add it
to the tin ball we were constructing. When it was large
as a basketball, he took it to be recycled for the war. I was five.

I didn't know what the war was, except that my father and uncle
listened to news and read the papers and discussed what
was happening in Europe. I don't know what they did
with those tin balls we constructed so carefully.
What I remember

is Zio Guillermo with his long slender fingers, artist's hands,
and the way they handled everything with such delicacy and grace.
He let me sit with him on his second floor porch while he carved
bird houses and whirligigs out of pine to decorate his garden.
He let me walk with him between the thick cornstalks in his garden,
the tassels of corn fine as silk, let me help him pick tomatoes and
peppers and zucchini. Zio Guillermo

was very quiet and reserved. Zia Louisa was tempestuous
and loud. She wore whalebone corsets to hold in her large
breasts and body. She loved to dance the Tarantella. She had
a little handkerchief, neatly ironed and folded, that she used to pat
away the sweat. She always yelled at Zio Guillermo. He'd hide from
her in the garden and pretend not to hear.

My mother said she'd hear Zia Louisa crying in the middle
of the night, but didn't know why. During the day, she was
the general; Zio Guillermo, the private. Even then, I wondered
why I felt sorrow coming off him in waves.

The day after he retired, he was walking back from Mastalia's
grocery store on the corner of 4th Ave; he collapsed
on the sidewalk and died. Though that happened
more than forty years ago, I can conjure
Zio Guillermo up, alive in my memory
as he was when we sat together creating

that tin ball, the smell of Camels filling the air around us
and I was his child to be cherished till I sparkled
like that silver ball in the dark.

When I Was Young We Played

When I was young we played Monopoly, my brother, sister and I,
and dominoes or gin rummy. We'd sit at our oil-cloth covered kitchen table
playing games after our homework was done or on weekend afternoons
in the winter. In summer, we played stickball in the street or hopscotch,
tossing a black rubber heel to mark our places. When we were really adventurous
we'd take our silver skates, tighten the clasps so they'd fit our shoes and we'd move
as fast as we could down 17th Street and onto 3rd Avenue until we reached
the slippery slate sidewalks in front of the shoemaker's shop, the sidewalks
that terrified me because when I reached them on those skates,
it felt like I was flying.

17th Street was its own small world. All our friends congregated there
either on the street or in the vacant lots with their daisies and Black-eyed
Susans. Sometimes we'd walk to the corner to Burke's candy store
for ice cream that Mr. Burke would scoop out of a vat into a small cardboard
container, and he'd give us a wooden spoon and we'd finish the ice cream
before we reached our front stoop.

On summer nights at dusk, a group of us would congregate on our back stoop,
and we'd try to catch fireflies in jars with holes punched in the lids and we'd "smoke"
punks to keep away the mosquitoes. We'd breathe in the tangy sweetness of Zio
Guillermo's garden, tomatoes, zucchini, eggplant, corn and pots of zinnias
and marigolds, and we'd tell stories there in the hushed summer dark.

Joey C's father set up a screen in their backyard and invited all the neighborhood
kids over to watch movies. Mr. C loved to see the kids have a good time and we did,
sitting in darkness, the sky still clear enough to see thousands of stars, the kids
lined up on folding chairs, others sitting cross-legged on the grass. The field
between Joey's house and mine sparkling with lightening bugs, the world
was as small and perfect as it would ever be, the net of happiness lifted
us out of our own skins, set us sailing above Joey's yard, above our ordinary
lives and away, even for a little while, from our mothers' voices calling us home.

We did not know then that for us this world would remain perfect and sealed
in glass like those globes that had inside them miniature villages,
and when you shook them snow fell through the air
like tiny falling stars.

In Second Grade

In second grade, Judy was my best friend.
Judy was the only blonde, blue-eyed Italian I knew.
She lived across the street from me and on the corner
of 17th Street and 3rd Ave in Paterson, NJ, the first floor
of her house was over a bar that her family owned.
Her grandparents opened the tavern right after Prohibition
ended and left it to their sons, Judy's father and two uncles,
to run. We'd get to her house by opening the gate in the chain link fence
into her overgrown backyard, past an enormous black cherry tree,
and to the back door, where we'd climb the steep stairs to her apartment.

Off Judy's kitchen, there was a covered porch that led to a huge terrace
that was actually the roof of the party room for the tavern, the room
they rented out for engagement parties and showers and weddings.
From up there, you could see our whole neighborhood and even lean
over the railing to see into the Riverside Oval, where we rode the swings
and seesaws and where the bigger boys played baseball. Sometimes, Judy

would come to my house but my mother was old-fashioned and strict
and I didn't have toys because my mother didn't think I needed them,
and Judy had a roomful of exquisite dolls and dollhouses given to her
by childless aunts and uncles. She was so beautiful, so like a china doll,
herself, that they couldn't resist spoiling her a little. We played for hours
with her dolls and doll furniture. The next year when we were eight,
her family bought a TV so all the neighborhood kids gathered in her living
room to watch Milton Berle in his silk hats or dressed as a woman
or the Little Rascals or Jack Benny. Judy's father was besotted with her,
bought her whatever she asked for, sent her to Benedictine Academy

instead of Eastside High School. Judy took the bus to Benedictine,
a private girls' school. That's where she met Billy and fell in love with him
though he went to Vocational Tech. One day I heard she had been
in an accident and broken her arm and dislocated her shoulder when Billy
was driving her home from a date. I went to visit her, though we had little
to say to one another by then, me, with my National Honor Society
and my head always stuck in a book, and Judy with her boyfriend
who wore a black leather jacket like the boys who hung out
on our street corner and always seemed so big and threatening.

When she was sixteen, she ran away to Maryland and married Billy.
Her father's hair turned white overnight. I heard gossip. Billy had broken
her arm and dislocated her shoulder. Billy had given her a black eye
and bruised her ribs. That was when she was still at Benedictine.
When the nuns asked her what happened, she'd say she walked into a door
or fell down the stairs. All the girls in her class knew.

Years later, she called. "I had five children with Billy, but he beat me up all
the time," she told me. "The last time he put me in the hospital for a month,
then I divorced him. I'm married again now to John. He's good to me.
But you know," she said, "sometimes, I miss Billy. He was so exciting."

My Fifth Grade Teacher Miss Spinelli

taught us kindness. I loved her for her dark
tragic eyes, for her hair as thick and curly
as mine, for her husky voice, reading stories
and poems, for the way she walked
down the dusty aisles of PS No. 18
and touched our shoulders
or the tops of our heads,
for choosing me to read aloud,
for encouraging me to write
though I was so shy I barely spoke.

In that classroom, she carved out a space
where I could be safe, where nothing,
not the shouting boys on the playground,
not the hatchet-faced principal,
not the petty meanness of the girls,
not the older boys in black leather jackets
could do me harm. I still see her looking

at me as though I were her beloved child,
her face, even after all these years,
wrapped in a veil of shimmering light.

Graduating from PS No. 18

In the photograph of our class in PS No. 18 in Paterson, NJ,
we are wearing our graduation dresses, the ones we sewed
ourselves, white eyelet with little cap sleeves and a nipped
in waist. We had to make our dresses in sewing class
and we took four or five months to finish them. Mrs. Z
taught us each step. By the time I finished it and brought it
home to be ironed, it was rumpled and filthy, the white dingy
and soiled. My mother had to take the dress apart and sew it
again but not before she washed it carefully by hand. "I had
to wash it three times," she said, "to get it clean."

In the photograph the dress looks fine. I am wearing a corsage,
one yellow rose, all the girls wearing the same flower. I am thirteen.
I called myself slim, but the others called me skinny or skinny bahlink.
I drank milkshakes to try to gain weight, but no matter how much I ate,
I weighed 94 pounds even with my shoes on.

In the photograph we all looked so fresh and hopeful, though what
did I know? How many were lonely or uncertain, how many afraid?
In our white graduation dresses we were what we were supposed
to be, looked the way we were supposed to look, while inside us all,
hope and terror trembled like small white birds.

I See Myself at Fifteen

I see myself at fifteen, white oxford cloth shirt, gray wool
skirt hanging past my knees, white bobby socks,
saddle shoes, so shy and uncomfortable in my own skin
that I am invisible. My sister with her Marilyn Monroe body
couldn't walk through a room without men staring.
I could have been a ghost for all the gazes that followed me,
my body pencil thin, my behind non-existent. That was
an era when women were supposed to have figures.

One of the girls in my class got pads for her hips in addition
to her padded bra. Today my granddaughter starves herself
so she is one, long, slender bone. I was ashamed of my body
or lack of it as I walked the halls of Eastside High School
in Paterson, New Jersey, those halls that terrified me
with their clumps of popular kids, loud boys and giggling girls,
all in on a secret I didn't know. I learned to hide, to keep my eyes
downcast, to choose the seat in the back corner hoping

no one would notice me. Even today, though I've read my poems
to thousands of people in Italy and Yugoslavia, read in amphitheaters,
in Macedonia on a bridge covered with white bunting where ten thousand
people lined both sides of the river, at a party I still choose a seat
in a corner and I don't move. I wait for people to come to me.

I pretend to be composed and satisfied. A few weeks ago I was too shy
to get up from the sofa and go into the dining room to help myself to food
so I sat there through the whole party, as hungry and uncomfortable
as I was when I was fifteen and I opened the waxed paper wrapped
around my spinach and oil sandwich on homemade bread, the aroma
of garlic rising around me at those worn wooden tables in the cafeteria
at Eastside, my head bent as everyone turned to stare. It is that girl,

so introverted she cannot speak, who has followed me my whole
life, that girl, who hides behind my bluster and courage,
my façade of power that deserts me the moment I am at a party
or in rooms crowded with people I don't know.

So Much That Is Not Right with the World

In the high school Home Ec class, Delores pushed
me and screamed, her face ferocious and untamed.
Thinking back, I can't blame her. How irritating
I must have been to her. I was the good girl,
the timid girl, the girl who never spoke.
She was the girl who was always twanging
with anger, her mother dead less than six months,
her father remarried to a woman she hated.

I was washing dishes in the sink in the small Home Ec
kitchen and she shoved me, and I was stunned
speechless. Not that I ever had much to say anyway,
but when she kept shoving me, I pushed her,
an ineffectual shove against such a big muscled,
athletic girl, a girl who hated everything I was.

The teacher stepped between us, called us
into her office, berated us both for fighting,
and I tried to explain myself, but she looked
right at me, her eyes hard and unforgiving.
I was sure she was going to have me expelled.

Later that week, through the bus window
I watched as Delores walked up the rickety steps
to her dilapidated house, watched as a woman
with disheveled hair reached out and snatched
her inside, pulling her by the hair and shouting.

Years later, I still remember Delores' eyes full
of shame and fear in that one moment before
the door slammed.

All His Life My Father Worked in Factories

or mills as we called them, back when Paterson
was the silk capital of the USA and was known as Silk City.
When my father was thirty he had a large tumor on his spine,
and after the doctors at St. Joseph's removed it
he spent three months in the hospital and then a year
at home. He couldn't work and wouldn't let my mother apply

for welfare so we lived for a year on $300, and while $300
in 1943 was a lot more than it is now, it still wasn't enough
for a family of five to live on. We ate spaghetti and farina
and my mother's homemade bread every day. When my mother
was dying, she worried that the year without money—
when she couldn't give my sister five cents to buy milk in school—
was why my sister got rheumatoid arthritis at thirty, a disease
that progressed, eventually invading her lungs and eyes.

After the surgery my father had a limp that became gradually
worse as he grew older. He was no longer strong enough
to lift heavy rolls of silk, so he got a job as a janitor
in Central High School and when that became too much
for him, he took a job watching the pressure
gauges on steam boilers to make sure they didn't explode.
All his life, my father walked, dragging that dead leg behind him.

All his life, he worked menial jobs, though he did income taxes
each year for half the Italians in Riverside by reading
the two hundred page income tax book, and he could add,
multiply and divide in his head faster than an adding machine.
He was fascinated by politics and read news magazines
and newspapers, and knew the details of world crises and war.

When I was a girl, I worked in factories during the summers
and I moaned and complained about how boring it was,
how dusty and tiring, how I'd shoot myself if I had to do this job
for one more day, and I think of my father with his sharp intelligence,

forced each day for fifty years to work eight hours a day at jobs
so repetitive they would have bored a mouse, and the way
he never complained, never said I can't do this anymore,
instead he just kept working, knowing he had to do it
so his children would have the soft lives he never had.

My Father's Tuba Disappeared

My father's tuba disappeared somewhere in my childhood,
though there is one picture of him holding the tuba
in his arms, wearing the gold epaulettes and fitted jacket
of his band uniform, proud in full sunlight, our tenement,
gray and seedy, in the background.

By the time I was old enough to notice, my father's tuba
had vanished into some locked closet, only the picture
to remind us that once he marched in that band
through the streets of Paterson, playing
booming tuba music and smiling.

Only now do I remember the gleam of that tuba,
the pride in his straight shoulders, and regret
that I lost this part of his life long before he died
at ninety-two, all that time when I could have asked him
when he stopped playing the tuba and why and what
happened to the gold braid of his uniform.

Girls

When people still called young women, girls,
and I was a girl, I lived by mother's rules.
"Good girls don't act that way," she'd say
and if I strayed from the lines she drew,

the lines I was always afraid to cross,
I could hear her voice telling me what
I could and couldn't do, like when
I fell in love with Brian

at first sight, his athletic body, all long-boned
grace, his handsome chiseled features,
his generous mouth, loved the way
I was comfortable with him right off, not shy
and tongue-tied as I usually was but rather

relaxed as if I had known him all my life, though
his father was a doctor and they lived in a huge
house in South Orange and you'd think, because
we lived in a tiny bungalow in Hawthorne that I

would have been intimidated by him, but no,
he'd hold my small hand in his larger one,
the fingers of his hand, long and slender, true
to his life as an artist and when he'd kiss me

it would light in me a fire I'd never felt before.
We were like those kissing dolls with magnets
in their lips so that we'd be drawn to one another
again and again, and he said he loved me and I

said I loved him and he said I want to marry you
and I said yes though I hadn't known him that long,
I thought I knew all I needed to know, but then,
he pulled away one night, "I have to tell you something,"

he said, and I could hear in his voice a forlorn sound.
"I was married, and I'm divorced.
I was only married a few weeks and she left.
Said she didn't want to be married," and I, hearing

my mother's voice, not even thinking to question
her ideas of what she thought a good girl should

do, a good Catholic girl and I did what her voice
told me to do, "No, I can't go out with you anymore.

You're divorced, I can't," and each time he called me,
I said the same thing, "No, I can't," though I wanted to,
though I would have eloped with him to Maryland if only
he hadn't been divorced, if only my mother's voice

would have let me, when I was still a girl, and my mother's
voice was the only one I dared to hear.

The Little General

My brother called our mother "the little general"
when we were teenagers, my brother driving

the car, my mother sitting next to him, her head
a small dark knob barely reaching the top of the seat,

my bossy mother who told us how to live our lives,
my mother who was always moving. When I

remember her, I see her almost as a blur,
like the cartoon of the road runner, my mother

who washed all the dishes as soon as the last bite
of food vanished from the plate, my mother who held

my doctor brother's foot until he fell asleep when he
was still a boy, my mother who sat at the kitchen table

with us, always ready to hear the stories of our lives,
ready to tell the story of hers, my mother who told me

everything that was wrong with me so I still hear her voice
though she said she told me for my own good,

my mother who loved the feel of the earth on her hands,
who smelled of flour and spices, who baked

thousands of loaves of bread, cooked innumerable
fragrant meals for her children and grandchildren

in her basement kitchen, my mother who taught me
how to laugh, my mother who could not read or write,

and though she wanted to go to school, my father
wouldn't let her, "Women don't need to go to school," he said,

my mother who did not know how much money my father
had in the bank and never wrote a check,

my mother who wanted to learn how to do
everything, my mother who could quote poems

she memorized in third grade in Italy before
she had to leave school, my mother who drew

an imaginary line around us to keep us close,
the front stoop our boundary, the family our country,

her little sturdy body better than any magic charm,
my mother whose skin turned orange before

she died, though the week before she got sick,
she planted a huge garden. We were sure

she was too powerful to die. Ma, even now,
ten years after the funeral procession led us

to Calvary Cemetery and to the mausoleum drawer
they filed you in, I wish I could drive over

to your house and find you there, your earthy humor,
your warm arms that always were the place

I call home.

My Mother Only Went to Third Grade in San Mauro

My mother only went to the third grade in Italy. In 1921,
that was when public education ended. In America,
she wanted to go to night school but my father said,
"No, women don't need to go to school."

My mother was ashamed that she never learned
to read English, but she was the one we all came
to for help, the woman who could figure out any
problem in a minute and a half, the woman who

always seemed huge and powerful in our eyes,
though she was only four foot eleven. When she was dying,
she talked about how much she wanted to go to school,
in her voice, regret and longing. She always seemed

so competent, able to figure out how to pave the driveway
or build the front steps or cure a broken heart. When I was
young, she couldn't help me with homework but she made
a space for me where I could do my work, let me read

at the dinner table because I couldn't bear to be parted
from my books, allowed me to walk alone four blocks
uphill to the local library each week though my mother
didn't like me to wander farther than the front steps,
encouraged my ambitions even when she thought
they were impractical for the daughter of immigrants

who needed to be able to support herself, bought me
a Smith Corona portable typewriter in a pink case
so that I could be the writer

I said I wanted to be.

Calling My Mother Back from the Dead

I am trying to see my mother now to bring her back
from the mausoleum drawer where we shelved her,
to bring her back, busy as always, heat rising off her body,
her arms pulling the wet sheet out of the wringer washer,
her body bending over the oven in the basement kitchen,
the aroma of roasting chicken and potatoes lifting into the room.

I am trying to see my mother now, the way she drove me wild
until I was forty when I suddenly understood with my own children
almost grown, the way she'd call me every day, ask after everyone
and hang up, no goodbye, no hello. I asked her once why
she didn't say goodbye and she said, "I call only to find out
you're all okay. That's all I need to know."

I am trying to see my mother now, her hand stroking mine,
my mother, the cinnamon and vanilla smell of her baking,
the basil and garlic that filled the air from the pots simmering
on the stove, my mother with the cups of espresso
she always had ready for us, those tiny china cups
and delicate spoons.

I am trying to call my mother back from the dead, retrieve
that kitchen that was so much a part of her, find solace
for these years that have been so filled with loss and ashes,
find again that place where she was always waiting.

February Day in Binghamton

To Maria and Mario Volpe and Giulia di Nicola

I look out the window at the endless mountains
on this bleak winter day, the mountains
a dark smudge against the sky.

Spring seems so far away, my bones
aching. I'm sure I'll never reach it, though
suddenly I remember San Mauro,

that mountain town in southern Italy
where my mother was born, that town
I saw for the first time with my daughter

this August, and for a moment I imagine
myself back on my cousin's flower-filled terrace
with its view of the town and the hills and the sea below,

the breeze so clear and smooth it could be water,
the days filled with espresso served in tiny cups
and homemade bread and tomatoes, and zucchini

with rosemary, and everything so delicately flavored,
so perfectly cooked, and most of all, the warmth
of these people, their smiles soft as sun on our faces,

the way a different life seems possible on that mountain,
and not the one I have, the one where I can't learn to say no,
the one where I'm too busy to sit outside, too busy to let

all the knots inside me unravel, too busy to gather for food
and talk the way we did when I was a child, Italian all around
me, its perfume heady as that of roses that climbed the back

porch trellis, those moments from the past I recapture
on that terrace in San Mauro and that return to me now
to warm me in this drab room on this February day.

Doing the Twist with Bobby Darin

One night I dreamt I was doing the twist
with Bobby Darin, but in fact of course,
I never did the twist at all with anyone.
I've always been shy in my body,
uncomfortable getting onto a dance floor
and moving wildly, even when I was
still young and thin.

Once when we were in grad school,
my friend's husband dragged me
out onto the dance floor, expecting
that I would be loose and easy,
imagining that all my energy
would translate into an abandon
I never felt when people
were watching. I understood

that he thought my Italian blood
meant I was hot like Sophia Loren
or Anna Magnani. He was disappointed,
and I was embarrassed, and when we went
back to the table to join my husband
and his wife, he never spoke to me directly
again, as though I had deliberately turned
stiff and uncomfortable because of him
and not because that's what
I've always been.

First Son

1.

I am in Dr. K's waiting room, I am two months pregnant
with my son. I hear Dr. K screaming at a woman in his office—
"I told you a soft boiled egg, you pig, you fat cow!" and I tremble
in my chair terrified that when I am in his examining room,
he will scream at me, though I was 107 pounds when I got pregnant,
119 when John was born. I am afraid of Dr. K who laughs at me
when I say I want to nurse my baby, and I am too cowardly
to stand up to him.

The Dr. K I know in that office is a sharp-tongued monster.
In the delivery room, while I struggle for 18 hours to deliver my son
who is a breech birth, Dr. K is kind, speaks softly to me. I hang onto
the bed rails, tell him I'm a coward. He says, "No, no, you're brave."
Medical students come in to stare at me. Dr. K's forehead is beaded
with sweat. When he finally slides the baby into the world, he shouts
as though he has just made a touchdown and says, "You're so beautiful,
I'm going to kiss you," but I turn my head so the kiss lands on my cheek
and I am embarrassed even now after all these years that my shyness
wouldn't let me accept his gesture as the kindness it was meant to be.

2.

When I first looked at my son, this boy we named John after Dennis'
father, I said, "Oh my, he looks like a monkey," his skin jaundiced,
his hair dark and wet on his big head. Dr. K said, "I'm insulted.
He's perfect. And look how long it took us to get him into the world."
I saw his dark skin, the huge raw patch on his scalp where the forceps
scraped away skin. I only saw an image of myself, dark-skinned, ugly
and it made me afraid. In a few days, jaundice gone, his skin
would turn fair, and by three months he was blonde and handsome
with big gray eyes, so good-looking people would stop me in the street
to comment. I always wondered whether they were thinking: "How did she
have such a beautiful child?"

3.

John is now almost forty-two. On Sunday, when I called him in Texas,
where he lives with his family, I can feel his unhappiness coming across
the wires, he tells me how much he hates Texas, tells me it's been raining
for days, all night thunder and lightning and he hasn't been able to find
another job so they can go back to North Carolina. His son is unhappy.
He misses his friends and has made no new friends in Dallas. His daughter
retreats into her books and her computer. His wife cries. He wants to be able
to fix the world, just as I do, and he can't fix this so easily. I can feel
his discouragement and know he feels that he isn't living up to his contract
as a husband and father, and I wish he were still that baby I held in my arms
in the chair where I rocked him through all those hacking, bronchial nights
in married student housing, holding him in my arms in that small room
with the humidifier until he stopped coughing and he slept. That time
when there was always something I could do to help him and not as I do now,
tears running down my cheeks while he talks, and I only have words
spoken over and over to soothe him.

Strange

Strange how some moments remain caught
in our memory, John at four on his new two wheeler,
his grandpa helping him until John took off and rode away.
It seems to me he's been riding away ever since,
first to college, then law school, then with his family
to Maryland, Virginia, North Carolina and now Dallas,
but as if it had happened yesterday, I remember
sitting on the side of his bed the night before
he started high school, his hand in mine,
while I found the words to give him courage
and with my hands, I smoothed over the turbulent lake
of his fear, until he was able to close
his eyes and fall asleep. I can see that room,
the bedside light casting shadows on the walls,
the books piled on the end table,
the thick lashes riding on the high curve
of his cheek, and I held his hand
and watched him sleep, knowing
this moment was one where I was learning,
what I'd learn again and again,
how to let him go.

The Cedar Keepsake Box

What happened to the cedar keepsake box my mother
bought me the only time I ever went to the Jersey shore
when I was growing up? After she told me that I couldn't have it,
too expensive, my mother bought it for me anyway.

"Here," she said, and turned away, my mother who loved us
with a devotion so complete we could have been saints
to her. I loved that box, loved the aroma of cedar,
rising out of it when I opened it. I loved the feel of the

burnished wood under my fingers, the box that would
keep my tender secrets for years. So much in our lives
is like that, we love and love and love an object
and then one day it disappears, and we don't notice as

though there was a canyon in the middle of the world where
all those lost loves go. It is like that with people, too.
So now, when I hear your voice on the phone, that
trembling, rasping it has become or when you tell me you

fell four times today and describe each place where you fell
or when you fumble for words to explain some simple fact,
I know you, too, are going to vanish
from my life, the smooth feel of your skin under my

hand, the way your shaking hands reach for me,
the same way I still remember the sweet smell
of cedar lifting into the air, the smooth feel
of that wooden box under my hand.

Was the Garden in Heaven or in San Mauro?

For years now my mother has been dead, fifteen years
since I held her hand in that hospital where her eyes
turned to milk glass and I knew she was gone. I hoped
to the perfect garden she described to me, that one filled
with light where she could walk with her mother and sisters
and I hope she is still there walking past incredibly perfect
flowers on a white stone path, arm in arm with the mother
she left behind in San Mauro, Italy, when she was twenty-three
and never saw again, and the sisters who died young.

I wonder if my sister and father have joined her, sunlight
caught in their hair, the air as perfumed as my mother's garden
in Hawthorne with the scent of rambler roses and tomatoes
and figs. I wonder if she is able to work the soil she so loved.
It is fifteen years since the white coffin with its stenciled flowers,
the parade of funeral cars to the Calvary Cemetery
and the mausoleum where she was placed, a metal box shoved
into a marble wall, the burial she wanted because she was afraid
we wouldn't take care of her grave and it's true that I never visit

that antiseptic building where her body is caught for eternity.
I cannot imagine, she who loved to work, her body moving so
fast through her life she was often a blur, can be contained
by that metal box. I refuse to release her, keep her alive
for myself and my children, telling stories about her, saying
the things she used to say, those pieces of San Mauro
she carried across the ocean with her, those pieces of that place
she gave to us so that when I go to San Mauro with my own
daughter, I am certain I have seen that perfumed place,
those people before, as though this is my hometown
instead of hers.

Even now, sometimes, I think she is with me. I feel her
behind me, turn toward her and for a moment she is there,
her hand held out to me, her arms ready to offer comfort
as they did when she was alive. Sometimes I catch myself
talking to her out loud when I am driving the car
and I can feel her presence warm as her hand on my face.

46

A Few Years Ago, I Moved You Out of Our Bedroom

A few years ago, I moved you out of our bedroom
into the room that had been our son's room
while he was growing up, moved you into a twin bed
and set the room up for you as though you were a teenager,
everything laid out exactly, your computer, your desk,
your reading lamp, your extra pillows, your blankets,
your clothes, carefully separated and in easy reach.

For years, we shared the mahogany four-poster
your mother left us, with its thick comforter
and flowered sheets and pillow shams,
but as your illness progressed, you were coming
to bed later and later, unable to lift your feet off the floor,
to move without falling or hitting the wall.
You'd wake me up from my deepest sleep
and then I'd be awake for an hour or two,
before I could fall back to sleep
and my alarm went off each morning at 6 a.m.

until I couldn't take it and though I am ashamed
of throwing you out of our bed, I tell you
it will be better for you and you can visit me
anytime you want and I repeat it will be better
for you, when I really mean it will be better for me.

I think back over the years we shared that bed,
the years when you were still healthy and strong,
when you slept in your summer pajama bottoms,
your chest naked, the blankets thrown off
because all that heat radiated off your body,
all the time that you took up most of the space
on the bed, while I trained myself to sleep
on my side at the edge so I wouldn't disturb you.

Only a few days ago, I realize I now sleep
on my side of the bed and yours, sleep
on both pillows, move restlessly in my sleep,

47

when I twist and turn and you are no longer there,
my body keeps searching for the space you used to
occupy, the heat of your body that warmed me
all those years when I was always cold.

The Other Night, You Came Home

The other night you came home from the church
where your friend took you to have your picture taken
for the parish book, I hear the scrich scrich of your wheelchair
on the kitchen tiles and then, you are next
to me, handing me a sheaf of photos. "I really look sick,

don't I?" you ask, and I scan the pictures and know
the camera has captured what neither one of us lets ourselves see,
that your illness is progressing so quickly that now even your face
looks delicate, the skin drawn

so tightly over the bones of your head that it's almost transparent,
your neck so thin it cannot support your head. Your eyes fix on me
and I know you need me to say it's not so bad. And I do, of course,
but the pictures offer such

solid evidence. How much of our conversation now
is based on lies, the lies I tell you so you won't know how you look;
the lies I tell myself so I won't have to know
how much worse you are now than even six months ago.

How complex it all is, how sometimes I want to excuse
my own desire to run away, to keep myself so busy I won't have time
to think about anything. I drag out things
you did to me forty years ago so I can be angry with you,

to excuse my own need, sometimes, to get in my car
and drive away from you, you in your electric wheelchair, you who
insist you can walk and fall so your legs and arms are marked by
bruises and scars, the way you scatter food

off your fork onto the floor, the slowness of each movement,
the excruciatingly long time it takes you to eat your dinner,
the way, sometimes, my impatience is an itch I can't scratch
for fear of hurting you, and the lies

have become the crutch I use to get through each day, the face
in my own mirror, one I can no longer stand to see.

All Morning in the September Light

All morning in the September light, I think of you,
imagine you struggling through your day while I sit
in the sun-washed classroom, that feeling
of being electric, as I am when I paint
or write a poem, my blood almost a chant
in my veins, every particle of my body alive.

All morning in the September light, I think of you,
how nothing stops you, not even this disease
that seems determined to rob you of everything.
You keep going to the Y to swim, even when
you can't swim without flippers, first
on your feet, then on your hands as well,
even when it takes you an hour to put on
your bathing suit and an hour to change again,
even when you can't use the dressing room anymore
because it is too difficult for you to get to the pool
from there, even when you have to change in an office
that is close to the pool, even when you have to wear
your bathing suit in the car and have the man
who drives you take you right to the edge
of the pool in a chair, even when the lifeguard tells you
that you can only stay in one small square of the pool
and you need a swimming buddy to watch you,
even when almost anyone else would have given up,
you keep on going anyway.

All morning in the September light, I think of you,
admitting to myself how impatient I've become,
my life so crammed with things I need to do
that I see you now in a blur, and I hear
in my voice what I don't say
aloud—*don't bother me now. I don't have
time for you,* so that at 3 a.m.,
in that bleakest hour, when I cannot sleep,
I allow myself to see what I have become,
my heart closed against you, my busyness
a mask I hide behind, my guilt a pill I cannot swallow.

April Snowstorm

It's April, but today snow starts to fall outside
the windows of this school where I have come
to be visiting poet, and where the students
with their incredible faces, delicate and strong
as calla lilies, try to write out the stories
they have to tell, and I am caught by the steady

snowfall and I think of you overwhelmed by this disease,
unable to take care of the simplest things because so often
you can't walk or even move your hand to operate your electric
wheelchair. Yet you went over to our neighbor who was selling
her glass and metal patio table and chairs, the one I wanted,
but would not buy because it seemed outrageous to spend
$2,000 on a table I wasn't even sure I'd ever use, but you
went over to the neighbor's house five or six times

in your wheelchair, wobbling and unsteady on your feet,
you rang the bell and asked if she was selling the table and then
came back and said, "Yes, $50," and I said, "Great" and you
went back again, because I felt too shy, and closed the deal.

When you return, I almost cry, thinking
this is why I love you, even after forty years,
this is how you show me you love me.

How Do I Pack Up the House of My Life?

Your voice on the phone last night, thin
and frightened, is a sound I hear in my bed

where I try to sleep. It is the shirt
I wear all day that torments me for having left

you behind while I bathe in the pleasure
of this new life, the horizons of my world

expanding. You tell me that at 2 p.m.,
your medicine stopped working. You have

not been able to move since then. It is now
nearly midnight. "It took me three hours to make

the shopping list," you say. "I'm afraid of what
will happen to me." And I hear the trembling

in your voice and the shame in my own heart
for the way my life is opening up. Yours

is slamming closed. There is no medicine
for the sound guilt makes at 3 a.m.

I cannot escape the picture of you in your
narrow bed unable to turn over and of myself,

here in this sunlit apartment where I pretend
that I am the only one who needs me.

I Conjure You Up

This morning, I drove away from home, leaving
Dennis behind. Dennis who is suddenly sure that a troop
of boy scouts or soldiers marched through the house,
certain that our daughter, Jennifer, who is in Cambridge
took him to the doctor's office, Dennis who is mumbling
to people none of us can see. "I'm in *Star Wars*," he says,
"I'm on a trip." His eyes are fogged over and lost.
"Dennis, Dennis," I say, "do you know who I am?"
Then, his eyes clear for a minute and he says,
"You think I'm crazy." Then they cloud over again.
This morning, I drive into sunlight and away
from the Jamaican woman who takes care of Dennis
when I'm gone, as I am so often. I drive
into Manhattan and down 68th street, past sun
dappled brick and brownstone, past city trees,
and to this school, where for awhile, I leave behind
the man I love and married so many
years ago, who soon won't know who I am.

I Was Thinking about Distances

driving through the Catskills
down miles of highway
and that made me realize
that the older we get,
the more alone we are.

So many things I can't say to you
anymore, so many thoughts
to hide in the pockets of my heart.
Remember when we went camping
in the mountains outside Taos?
We were so young driving up

the side of those steep mountains
and when we reached the top,
the muscles in your arms straining
against the pull of the wheel, afraid
that the VW bus wouldn't make
it to the top, cursing at it because
you were worried the VW would roll

backwards down that mountain.
And, finally, at the crest of the road,
we passed into a grove of birch trees
as though New England had appeared
above the red sand and desert
landscape of New Mexico, the knots
in my clenched hands loosened
and I could breathe again.

Later, under a sky crammed with stars,
we sat near the campfire after the children
fell asleep in the tent. I can still
smell the baby powder and shampoo
of their skin and hair. The air grew cold
as soon as the sun went down. Remember,

how we wrapped up together in a blanket near
the fire, how you were the best friend
I had ever had, how I would tell you anything?
I was happy just to sit next to you, your arm
around me, my shoulder touching your shoulder,
my arm your arm. How lucky we were, in our
mid-twenties, just out of grad school, our interest

in books and theater and art and movies
meshing like the fingers of our hands

linked together. And today, so much to hide.

When I Got Married, I Thought I Knew Everything

When I got married, I thought I knew everything, the words
of the ceremony clear as a knife, the "in sickness and in
health" part of the ritual we believed would be easy, no
understanding of what we were promising or how difficult it
could be, how lonely, as your illness confines you more
and more in a body that is breaking down, a mind that
seems cloudy and unsure, while I try to pull our house,
complete with nurse's aides and medicine and
wheelchairs, behind me like a huge red wagon, try to keep
you balanced and moving forward, even as my own body
reacts with migraines, arthritis. That promise I made so
many years ago gets harder and harder to keep, though I
know how much you need me, know my love for you is
stronger now than it was years ago when I trembled in my
white dress and walked toward you down the aisle of St.
Anthony's Church and the only thing I saw was that you
were the beautiful man I loved. When I looked at you my
breath caught in my throat, and even today, your face
marred by disease, your body weak and trembling, the you
I love is there in the way you hold my hand to your cheek,
the way you smooth back my hair.

Jacobs Department Store

When I was growing up, we'd go to Jacobs Department
Store in Paterson, New Jersey, my mother, brother,
sister and I made our way to the shoe department
to get our shoes. They carried brown oxfords, Buster
Brown, the only name brand item my mother ever
bought for us. No ballerina shoes for us. Only those
chunky oxfords, trying to insure our feet would be as
safe as she tried to keep us. In the shoe department,

they had a machine that x-rayed your feet so they
could fit you with the perfect size shoes. I loved that
machine, sliding my feet into it so I could see the bones
in my feet, the shape of them like silver shadows. How
easy it was to see the interior of the foot, the bones
of the toes, but today nothing is easy. I'd like to slide my
life into that foot measuring machine, figure out why on
a day so bright with autumn, my worry is darker than

all beauty and nothing is easy. Not the email I get
from my son in Texas saying, "I don't want to talk
about it, but Texas stinks," and I know my son, a man
of few words, has sent out a distress call louder
than a sonic boom, and if I ask him, he won't tell me
what's wrong, though he used to tell me everything
when he was a boy and I sat on the side
of his bed and held his hand until he fell asleep
and nothing is easy, not my worry about my husband

whom I left behind yesterday even though
his head is bent sideways on his neck
so it looks as though he's going to hit doorways
and walls and often does, not my guilt that when
I went to bed the other night I heard him cursing
and shouting, and I heard the aide who now lives
with us because he can't be left alone, go downstairs,
and I fell asleep anyway, and my guilt when the aide

tells me the next morning that he was trying to get
to the bathroom and he fell and wet his pants
and she had to calm him down and change his clothes
and wash him, the way I did so many times
before she moved in and I am ashamed
that I have hired someone else to do
what I can't manage anymore. I don't need
that foot machine to see how devastated and broken
the lines of my life have become, and no shoes, no shoes
to fix what is wrong.

How Spring Turns

Each spring I fall in love again with the sun's
hand on my face, the way the trees, still caught
by winter's frost, soften and bud, though last week

it snowed so much the university had to close
for the day, while in New Jersey it rained so long,
the bridges flooded and the river even buried Libby's

Famous Hot Dogs, a popular luncheonette that's been
in the same spot on the Passaic River since I was a girl.
Today none of that matters because this April day it is

suddenly, amazingly, spring and for the first time in days,
I don't feel alone. How can we tell anyone
what we confront each day? Who would care

even if we could find the courage to tell? I remember you
sitting at the dining room table when I was trying
to get ready to leave to drive up 17 west to Binghamton

and just minutes before, you fought with Ethelyn,
the Jamaican woman who is taking care of you
because you can't be left alone. Our basement flooded

when it rained and she's yelling that there are germs
down there and you can't go to your study, the room
you built for yourself years ago when you were still healthy.

You scream at her, "You're not my boss. Don't talk to me
like that," and your whole body is twanging and I step
between you two, try to get you to calm down, tell her that

you can go back down to your study by Saturday,
get you to agree, though you mutter that you hate being
treated like a child, that you hate being useless.

"What kind of life is this?" you say. Before I leave,
I put my arms around your neck, press your head
against my chest, and kiss the top of your head.

After all these years together, I know that you understand
the language of my touch, the comfort I place
like a china cup in your open palm.

A Poem about a Turnip

I could write a poem about a turnip or a sweet potato,
but what good would it do? My ex-son-in-law, the one
who hurt my daughter so badly that I don't know
if she'll ever recover, served me turnips once. I hated them,
so white, bland and difficult to swallow like his betrayal,

his words. "I've met someone else. I want a divorce."
I imagine my daughter standing in their small apartment,
her face shocked silent, her eyes filling with tears.
"You're beautiful," he tells her. "You'll find someone else."

She comes home to me, walks into my arms and sobs.
We spend that entire weekend crying, though I try
to hide my tears from her, even as she soaks my shirt
with her own. I'd hit my ex-son-in-law in the head
with a turnip or a really big uncooked sweet potato
if I could.

I think of my daughter so distraught that year that she drove
into the back of her friend's car, that she tells me she dreamt
Paul was in bed with her, dreamt he had come back
and then he said he changed his mind and vanished.
She woke up sobbing. We were together eleven years,
she tells me, eleven years, and then she starts to pretend

it doesn't matter, pretend that it never happened, pretend
that she is happy being alone. Whenever I think of turnips,
I think of him, the mask he wore around us that made me believe
he was my son, the letters he wrote to me after they divorced
saying he wanted to be my friend, the way he shook off
their eleven years together and went on with his life.
Behind his handsome face, his loving smiles,

there hid another face, ugly and unfeeling,
as the turnips he served so proudly.

Forgetting to Give Thanks

I watch the public TV program on Rwanda
and the water they are lifting out of polluted
wells to drink, though there's a cholera epidemic.
It is the only water they have and they draw
a pail of it out of the well. The water is brown
and thick and muddy. The emaciated man
walks away with the pail of water.
Several children walk behind him.
They stop at the side of the road
and the man lets each of them drink
from a battered metal dipper.

In my house I forget to give thanks
for the clean water that pours
out of the kitchen faucet, the water
in the bathrooms, hot and plentiful,
for long showers and baths.

We forget how much of the world does not have
what we have and even I forget, I who grew up
in an apartment heated by a coal stove. The only warm
place was at the kitchen table set up close to the stove.
The bedrooms were frigid. My mother would warm
the beds with bricks she heated in the oven
and then we'd rush in and jump into bed.

The house had no insulation and no storm windows,
so the windows would develop a coating of ice
in patterns I thought were beautiful. We bathed in water
that my mother heated on the stove. My mother washed
our clothes on a tin washboard.

Today, with my house full of appliances—stove,
refrigerator, dishwasher, washing machine,
dryer, air conditioners, TV's and as much
hot or cold water as I want—I forget to be grateful,
and am only reminded for a minute when I see
those people in Rwanda who are drinking water
so filthy it will probably kill them. Or when I think
of my mother and all the work she did, carting
buckets of coal, stoking the fire, boiling water
to keep us warm.

In My Dream, the Light

In my dream, the light in the room turns
into a disco ball—blue / red / yellow / green,
the colors spastic and startling.

My father crouches in the corner.
He smiles at me but when he speaks
I cannot understand him
because he has taken out his teeth
which float in a glass on the window sill.

The lights pulse and waver.
My mother is in the room with me.
It becomes her kitchen, that basement
kitchen with the old Kelvinator refrigerator.
She reaches in pulling out dish after dish of pasta—
lasagna, *braciola*, roasted chicken and potatoes,
but when she turns around, it is not my mother at all,

but someone with huge dark circled eyes and a bright
red gash of a mouth and huge stitches bisecting
her face and body, as though someone had cut her
in half and sewn her back together, and the dishes
on the table are full of severed heads and pulsing
hearts. Though I want to get away, there is no place
left that is safe, no place to run and hide.
I cannot look at the severed heads, the pulsing heart,
the body stitched together with orange thread,
I cannot look.
I cannot get away.

My friend writes that her cancer is back
and it's in her bones. She has to have radiation and chemo
again. My friend, who is the same age as I am, looks 20 years
younger. My friend wants me to tell her she will survive
and be cancer-free. The creature in my dreams opens
her lipsticked mouth and becomes a wolf, bares her fanged teeth,
howls and howls at the moon.

In These Green Mountains

In these green mountains, the music
of the universe is everywhere,
I can hear it:

In the weight of snow on evergreens;

In the song of daffodils waiting under
the black earth for spring.

In these green mountains, the music
of the universe heals
all that is gray and broken,
all that is bleak and betrayed.

How it soothes us and we sigh
as it fills all the spaces inside us
that for so long have been silent and empty.

Only this clear scented air,
the feathery green of the trees,
can carry the music of the universe,
the song that birds know.

A Man Stands over My Bed

Last night, I woke up at 3 a.m. and find
a man standing near the head of the bed,
a youngish man, maybe mid-30s, thin,
almost gaunt with beady black eyes
and a scraggly moustache and a black denim jacket.
I expect to find you in my room, not this stranger
who looks vaguely sleazy and shifty and who seems
to want something from me. When he is gone,
and I am alone in the semi-darkened hotel room,
the unfamiliar furniture forms shadows in the corners
and against the walls. I have been sleeping on our sofa
for months now. After I broke my shoulder,
I slept in a recliner for weeks and then on the sofa.
Your ashes are in a wooden box surrounded by pictures
of you when you were young, pictures of us together
when you could still travel. In those weeks, the painkillers
always stopped working at 3 a.m. and I'd wake up
and know you were there in the room with me.
I'd talk and you'd listen, seeking comfort from you
though you died in May and I didn't even have
the courage to place your ashes in the box
but instead asked my daughter to do it. And if I'm honest
with myself how could I ask you
to come back to me, you who in those last weeks
were sure you were in *Star Wars* or *Peter Pan,*
you whose hands turned black, and gangrenous,
you who were so thin even the smallest diaper
no longer fit you. We would have been married
forty-seven years in June, but you died in May.
I'm glad I now sleep in this room where your ashes rest,
where I can apologize to you for the way I ran away
from everything I could not face about the illness
that crucified you. In the 3 a.m. dark
I swallow the pills to soothe the ache of my bones
as they try to heal, and I imagine you hold my hand
and watch over me while I sleep.

Festival at Northern Valley High School

Outside the window the sun turns the world
bright, the dappled leaves of the trees reflected

in the aluminum walls of the school, the pile
of rocks in the courtyard still dabbled with snow,

first day in what seems like weeks that the sun
is out. Spring is a promise I know can't be kept

on this fourth day of February, two months
of gray days ahead of us but today I can imagine

that it is already spring, the students at the festival
sitting in a circle around me, their faces concentrating

on the movement of their pens on white paper.
My eyes drawn away from them to the snow-

spattered landscape outside the window
and drawn back to them, their sneakered feet,

their backpacks, gray and black, blue and tan
scattered on the floor, the boys willing to write

about their dogs and mostly afraid to write
about themselves or their lives. Sometimes they look

directly at me and I see behind their cool façade,
their blasé looks, the person inside, fragile
and uncertain, yearning to be understood.

Life Was Simple

Life was simple when I could sit with my children
on my lap and read to them, the two of them
always wanting one more book, one more.
Life was simple when I planted morning glories
on the chicken wire fence at the Quonset hut we lived in
at married student housing at Rutgers, and the sandbox
my mother-in-law bought for John so he could play
with his pay loaders and dump trucks. Life was simple
when my son could sit for hours in the wicker
clothes basket and play with his matchbox cars,
whispering stories to himself.

Everything changes. Nothing is simple now.
John living with his family in Dallas.
Jennifer alone in Cambridge.
I, left behind in the house my husband and I
lived in together for nearly forty years before he died.
My grandchildren almost grown up, my grandchildren
who barely know me, though I fly down to visit,
write emails. My son has trouble finding what to say
to me, my generous, handsome, kind, efficient son
who tries to visit me for a few hours when he is on
a business trip to New York, but who cannot quite meet
my eyes and who thinks that I should give up my poetry
and workshops and readings all over the world,
who looks at me as though he doesn't know anything
about me, and I wonder, does he remember the hours
I read to him, the moments when we were so close
that it was like we were one skin?
My daughter called me the other day
to say, "I wanted to tell you that you are a really
good mother," and I wonder what my son
would say if he could hear her.

When I Speak Sometimes

When I speak sometimes
I hear my mother's voice
though she's been gone 20 years.
I can't resist taking care
of the world,
I who find myself
giving unasked for advice
like my mother,
I who sometimes
think I can do everything,
know everything,
remember how annoyed
I was when my mother
would tell me what
I was doing wrong
and why her way was better
than mine, become her
when I give my son
advice he doesn't want
or need, my son
who, though he doesn't know it
now, is me, the one
who takes care of everyone,
the one his family goes to
for advice and comfort,
my son who takes his nineteen-year-
old daughter out for a long ride
so they can talk who tells
her, "You shouldn't let
any boy treat you like that,
you deserve to be treated
like a princess," my son
who despite a busy week
at his law firm, a week in
which he travelled to California
and back in the same day, so he
wouldn't be away from his family,

my son who spent so many weekends
this year backpacking up a mountain
with his son and the boy scout troop,
sleeping in a tent,
my son whom I so annoy,
my son who is just like me,
though he would deny it
and refuses to recognize
when he speaks sometimes
it is my voice he hears.

Why I Worry

My granddaughter is 19. She is a freshman
at a huge university. She is lonely. "I've made no friends,
grandma," she tells me. I tell her to talk to people
in her classes. To smile at people. To join a club.

My granddaughter is five feet eight,
weighs 104 pounds. If she eats something,
she has to exercise for an hour.

My granddaughter's looks are striking.
She has dyed her hair auburn,
has huge blue eyes, wears dramatic eye makeup
and loves to create outfits. She wants
to write for a fashion magazine or blog.

My granddaughter has to get all A's.
She studies and studies and does extra work.
My granddaughter needs to be perfect,
needs to be the best at whatever she does.

I try to make her realize how beautiful she is,
how creative and intelligent, but for now,
the voice inside her, that crow, is louder than mine.

The Boys Call My Grandson Names

I carry my grandson's picture
in my wallet now as though by carrying him
with me I could make the boys in his junior
high stop calling him names.

In the picture he has his arms folded
across his chest as though that would prevent
people from noticing the weight he's gained
in the same way I wear black

hoping that I will hide the obvious fact
that I am no longer 104 pounds. His mother
tells me that often when she picks him up
from his new school in Texas, he is crying.

His best friend from North Carolina still calls
him every week. They spend an hour
on the phone together and I hear in his voice
how happy he is when he talks

to him, how words spill over themselves
as he talks. When he hangs up, he goes up
to his room and does not come out for an hour.
I know that for the rest of his life,

he will remember the names those boys call him,
the names he is too ashamed
to repeat to his mother and father, though
they ask him: what is it? what is it?

He refuses to say. I think of those wood burning kits
you can use to burn a name on a cabin or a door,
and I know that the names they called him are burned
in his memory in letters as thick and dark as any

you could hang on a door and he will carry those voices
with him, even when he is old and has lived his life,
the way we all remember the first time other children
pointed at us and laughed and the loneliness

of a junior high field where no one picks you for a team
or calls you friend.

The Riots in Cairo

Outside the window, snow swirls from the sky.
Students run across the quad in sweatshirts.
Two minutes ago the sun was out. Now

it looks like Alaska. In the newspaper photo, thousands
of people are rioting in the streets. So many people
crowded together, it almost looks as though they are
standing on each other's shoulders.

When I was nineteen, I went to Times Square
on New Year's Eve with Chuck, the boy
whose last name I've forgotten though he was the first boy
I slept with. The idea of Times Square
on New Year's Eve excited me, but being there
I thought I'd suffocate—my face shoved against
the jacket of a man who was at least six-feet tall,
whose shoulders were wide as a building.
I wanted only to get out but there was so much noise
that Chuck didn't hear me, people in front of me
and in back and on the side, terror sharp as tin in my mouth.
I look again at the photos of the riots in Cairo and wonder

if in those crowds, there's a girl who finds herself, suddenly
wanting only to escape all the people, pushing
and pulling around her. The rioting has been going on for days.
What little it would take for the riots to spread to other places,
for the Middle East to blow up.

We sit in this classroom, protected by warmth and brick from the snow
outside the windows, from the riots and bloodshed and famine
that roar through so many parts of the world,
while we, with our snacks and pill bottles, our safe skins,
don't know enough to be grateful for everything we have.

The Bratz Dolls Outpace Barbie

Today I read in the newspaper that Bratz dolls
are rapidly replacing Barbie as the top selling doll
in the world. Bratz dolls are dressed in skimpy skirts
and sequins, faux fur, platform shoes and bare midriffs.
They look like the women who used to wait for men
to pick them up on 42nd street outside the Lincoln Tunnel
and here they are in little girls' bedrooms all over the world.
I remember when Jennifer played with her Barbie dolls,
dressing and undressing them, she and Kimmie, her best friend,
making up stories for them, ones in which Ken was handsome
but not as important as Barbie, Barbie's Dream House
and Barbie's Camper, and Barbie's pink sports car, instead of

Bratz dolls with names like "Express It" and "A Go-Go,"
and while Barbie wanted to be a nurse or a teacher,
what can Bratz girls possibly do except
the oldest profession on earth?

I imagine little girls around the world making up stories
about those Bratz dolls. Will they imitate them when they start
to grow up? And I remember suddenly Jennifer
at thirteen who said she wanted to be a model

so I said, "I'll take you to New York to a modeling agency,"
and I did. Jennifer is dressed in a sweater and slender slacks
and high heels and we're crossing 5th Ave together.
I see men staring at her and I am ashamed of how clueless I am,
sometimes. How could I have allowed her to leave the house
dressed like that? These men think she's a call girl and their eyes,
hot and knowing, follow her. I cross my fingers and hope
she doesn't notice them watching. Years later, she takes
my 15-year-old granddaughter, tall and slender and blonde, to the city,
my granddaughter who is still a little girl inside and who wears

a trendy short skirt that shows off those long, slim legs of hers
and Jennifer says, "Oh, men were staring at Caroline," and I know
she had the same reaction I did, when I saw the way men looked at her.

And now I read about these Bratz dolls and find out they're made
in Chinese sweat shops where workers earn $4.13 a day, less than
the price of one doll, work in shops without health insurance, sick days,
so that we can buy these dolls that teach our daughters how to love
all that glitters and shines.

In Japan, the Earthquake

The TV newscaster shows scenes of Japan
after the earthquake and tsunami. Flashing
across the bottom of the screen, *Japanese*
concerned about the meltdown of a second reactor.
The Japanese evacuated the area for twelve miles
around the reactor. The air is already contaminated.

How easily we break, and once broken, how
can we be repaired? My daughter, even eight years
after her husband told her he met someone else
and wanted a divorce, has not healed. She trusts
no one. Retreats to the safety of her condo.

My daughter is still broken. I wish for her a daughter
like the one she has been to me, but even I, the optimist
of all optimists, no longer allow myself to believe.

In Japan, the nuclear reactor melting, the air contaminated,
they evacuated the area for twelve miles. It is already too late.
They say they tested people and though they test positive
for radiation, they're not sick yet. I look at the picture
in the newspaper of a grandmother with her grandson
after the evacuation. She has her arms around him,
he leans into her chest. Imagine all the people who will die
from radiation, maybe not tomorrow or the next day but soon.

My daughter has been touched by the radiation
of her husband's betrayal. She is only one person,
and though she is mine, I know that the world is full
of destruction. The TV announcer says the same thing
that happened in Japan could happen here—Indian Point
so close to huge centers of population. But we are Americans.
We believe we are invulnerable. We believe we are safe.
We are certain nothing like that can happen to us.

That night, my daughter's husband told her,
"I have something to tell you and you're not going to like it."

But in the moments before his words hit her like bullets,
she did not suspect. She cooked dinner, washed the dishes,
hummed under her breath. She thought nothing bad
could happen to her, the man she loved in the living room,
she in the kitchen humming. The people in Japan
were going about their lives, while radiation seeped
into the air around them and they breathed it in.

Here in This Gray Room

To my poetry students at Binghamton University

Here, in this gray room, we sit
around a long, gray table
and write our poems.

When we read them to each other,
the room becomes quiet with the kind of stillness
usually only found in deep woods.

This is a safe place we've come to,
a place where all our scars can be revealed,
a place where we can put down our sorrow

like a basket full of stone,
a place where we can cry and others
will pass us tissues and cry with us,

a place where we, with our one less layer
of skin, we who are so aware of our own flaws,
can tear away the veils

we hide under in the ordinary world,
veils as thick as the burka
that Muslim women wear.

My Friend Reads to Her Children

My friend reads the story of *Beauty and the Beast*
to her two little girls, Caelan, five, and Keene, two.
Keene is dressed in a Princess Belle outfit, all pink
and sparkly. A tiara sits on her curly blonde hair.
Caelan is suddenly a grown up little girl, articulate
and solemn and sensitive. They both listen
and comment while my friend reads. I listen, too,
and enjoy the theatrical quality of my friend's voice.

When I was a child, my parents didn't speak English
so they couldn't read stories to me, though my mother
would sit us in the padded rocker next to the coal stove
that heated the apartment, and tell us Italian folk tales
that were as mesmerizing and frightening as Grimm's
grimmest tale. In grammar school teachers read stories
to us. I loved the sound of the story read out loud by

someone for whom English was a first language, and then
one day I turned the dial on the radio and heard *Sleeping
Beauty* read aloud by an actress. I loved hearing the story,
the way the words drew me into a world far removed from
that Paterson kitchen and every week after that, I'd sit
for an hour, listening to another story read by the actress
with the beautiful voice. I sit next to Caelan when her mother

reads and I remember sitting with my son and daughter
in my arms so many years ago, and I am gratified
for the blessing of these children, the way they reach out
their arms to me when I arrive, the way they quarrel over
who will sit next to me, the way when Caelan puts her arms
around me, my own daughter at four comes alive for me again,
and the child I was, and sometimes still am, floats

into the story, the way I did when I listened to the radio
in that 17th Street apartment while the coal stove crackled
and sparked and the language was smooth and comforting
as satin on my skin.

The Ducks Walk across River Street, Paterson, New Jersey

Yesterday, a family of ducks crosses River Street.
All the cars, in both directions, stop to let them go by,

their black heads proud in the air, their beaks pointed
ahead, straight and self-satisfied. They do not hurry.

They walk as though they own the world, two grown
ducks, three ducklings, two more ducks taking up the rear.

You'd think they lived on some curvy lane
in the English countryside, somewhere near Wordsworth

Cottage perhaps, instead of on the Passaic River, reeking
of garbage, redolent of waste, near the edge of River Street

with its thrift shop and boxing gym and car wash
and its gaggle of homeless men who sit in broken down

chairs on the edge of the river, as though they, too,
were at some expensive resort. How self-contained

the ducks are, all of us watching them, the people
in their cars heading to work, the homeless men

mumbling or staring at the trees trailing their long fingers
in the river, the ducks certain in their smooth feathers

that the road and the river are theirs by right
as they move graceful as dancers onto the water

and let it lift them into the dazzling morning light.

CPSIA information can be obtained at www.ICGtesting.com
Printed in the USA
BVOW010700200213

313714BV00001B/9/P